It's Medieval!
A Kid's Guide to Nuremberg, Germany

Photography By John D. Weigand
Poetry By Penelope Dyan

Bellissima Publishing, LLC
Jamul, California
www.bellissimapublishing.com

Copyright © 2013 by Penny D. Weigand and John D. Weigand

All rights reserved. No part of this book may be reproduced or transmitted in any form or by any means, electronic or mechanical, including photocopying, recording, or by any other means, or by any information or storage retrieval system, without permission from the publisher.

ISBN 978-1-61477-079-4
First Edition

"All truly great thoughts are conceived while walking"

Friedrich Nietzsche

1844~1900

It's Medieval
Bellissima Publishing, LLC

Introduction

Nuremberg, Germany is the second largest city in the State of Bavaria; and Nuremberg tries hard to shake off its Nazi past and the formerly well-publicized Nuremberg Trials. They have a magnificent Christmas Market that has been known to bring in thousands of tourists. However, the best thing about seeing Nuremberg today is its medieval past is clearly visible nearly everywhere! You can walk over a bridge through an archway to a medieval shopping area; and you can see all sorts of fun things in this city just by taking a walk and taking a good look around, and this is exactly what kids like to do!

Written in verse by award winning author, attorney and former teacher Penelope Dyan, with photography by former television director of engineering, John D. Weigand, this book is a delight to the eyes. And to make things even better, you can use this book to practice early reading skills because the verse is based on word recognition and rhyme, so kids can shout out what is coming next. This is a book that teaches about using the mind and the senses, not a book filled with boring facts. Weigand and Dyan see through the eyes of a child; and as a former teacher, Penelope Dyan seems to just know what a child sees and wants to see.

It's Medieval!
Bellissima Publishing, LLC

It's Medieval!
A Kid's Guide To Nuremberg, Germany

Photography By John D. Weigand
Poetry By Penelope Dyan

When you go to Nuremberg
and walk down the street
the cobblestones fly
beneath your two feet,
unless (of course) of feet
you have four,
and THEN the cobblestones
fly even more!

You can see the world
as once it stood,
made so beautifully
of stone and wood.

There is a stone tower
that reaches so high,
you fear it might pop a hole
in the winter morning white sky!

And as you walk down
another colorful street,
you spy fruit and vegetables
ripe and ready to eat.

Your tummy grumbles
and you wish
you could go inside this place
and eat some fish.
But when you look
at this smiling head,
you decide you'd rather have
bratwurst and sauerkraut instead.
Or maybe you'd like
some wiener-schnitzel,
like you had once long ago
when you were little!

You walk across a bridge
and through a castle-like door,
and you know beyond these walls
you'll see even more!

You bounce along down
a dark and mysterious walk.
You are so captivated by it,
that you can hardly talk.

Through THIS archway
you watch people come in and go out,
and once they're inside
they just look about!

You see a shop with
lots of toys and stuff,
and then if that is not enough...

You see some painted wooden birds
that are very, very funny.
You ask, "Are they for sale?
And do they cost much money?"
Your mother looks them over, and says,
"I don't think they're for sale my son,
but they certainly ARE
a WHOLE lot off FUN!

And then as the street
lights get ready to light up the sky,
you know that it's time to say good-bye;
or at least it's time to say good night,
because to stay up TOO late
would just NOT be right.

Then as you walk
along the castle wall.
Your mother says, "You've had a ball!
But soon it will be time
to go to bed,
and on a feather pillow
rest your head.
So, let's find a restaurant
and get something to eat,
where I can sit down
and rest MY feet!"

Oh, yet we trust that somehow good
Will be the final end of ill,
To pangs of nature, sins of will,
Defects of doubt, and taints of blood;

That nothing walks with aimless feet;
That not one life shall be destroyed,
Or cast as rubbish to the void,
When God hath made the pile complete

FROM IN MEMORIAM A.H.H.
LORD ALFRED TENNYSON